Are You A Network Marketer Or Nah?

By: Vanisha Alexander-Marshall

OVERVIEW

This is an overview of what we feel network marketing should be about. We hope after reading this book that you have a better understanding of network marketing or for those people that are in the network marketing world a better idea of how network marketing works and hopefully have an idea of how to run a better, smarter, more efficient home based business.

DISCLAIMER FROM THE AUTHOR

This is strictly based on personal experiences combined with research done by myself. I do not feel the experiences I have gone through will be the same experiences you will endure during your network marketing experience. Please be advised this is only based on personal experiences and research.

Are You A Network Marketer Or Nah?

By: Vanisha Alexander-Marshall

CHAPTERS

Chapter 1

The True Meaning of Network Marketing

What is network marketing? Really, what is the true meaning of network marketing and what does it entail? Honestly, if you want to know the dictionary meaning of network marketing, it is defined as "a business model in which a distributor network is needed to build the business. Usually such businesses are also multilevel marketing in nature in that payouts occur at more than one level" ("Network Marketing" entrepreneur.com).

Network marketing can also be defined as a "direct selling method in which independent-agents serve as distributors of goods and services, and are encouraged to build and manage their own sales force by recruiting and training other independents agents. In this method, commission is earned on the agent's own sales revenue, as well as on the sales revenue of the sales-force recruited by the agent and his or her recruits (called downline)" ("Network Marketing" businessdictionary.com).

In a nutshell, network marketing is simply partnering with a company that offers products or services and you are a representative that is building a business using the company's name, products and/or services. It is very similar to building your own franchise McDonald's or Burger King, but you are building your own franchise from network marketing standpoint.

Network marketing has many similarities like any traditional business owner. For example, just like any business, you need people to build your business. In this case, the people that will help build your business will be called your business partners or recruits. Even though these new people in your business are helping you build your business, they are looking to you to help them build their business as well. These new business partners will be your backbone in sustaining your business just like any employee would be when you first open the doors to your new store front or your whatever new business you begin. However, just like you have brought someone into your business, someone brought you into their business (also known as your upline). Remember, your upline in depending on you to sustain your business so you can sustain their business (also known as multilevel marketing). Everyone is looking to win in their network marketing business and no one wants to fail. The best way for everyone to win and be successful and work together.

Chapter 2

Can You Really Handle Network Marketing?

When people first get into the world of network marketing, the first question that most people never ask themselves is can they really handle network marketing? Think about it for a moment. When you are first introduced to an opportunity, you are so excited about it and you are ready to get started and begin making money with your new network marketing business but we tend to fail in our mindset if network marketing really in our bones. When someone is bringing a network marketing opportunity to you, what is your mindset when you first see it? Are you really believing that you can do this business called network marketing? Can you really bring people into your network marketing business? It may look attractive to you but when the real work comes in, your mindset starts to come in and tell you this is not the business for you and you simply quit doing your business. Then your upline will start calling you wondering what's going on with your business and why haven't you done anything. It is simply because you thought in the beginning you could handle this business called network marketing but in the end, you realized you could not handle it.

The biggest reason people cannot handle network marketing is because they cannot deal with the word "no." When you get started in your network marketing business, you are so excited to share your business opportunity. However, the first thing you tend to hear is the word "no." After a while of being in business, you will hear so many no's that you begin to believe that network marketing is not the business for you and you simply cannot do it. This is when your mindset comes into play and you really begin to wonder can you handle network marketing? Will your mindset allow you to handle the ups and downs of network marketing? It is up to you to absorb the word "no" and move on and think "yes I can do this business." If you continue to let "no" win in your mindset, you will never be successful not only in network marketing, but in life.

Another reason people cannot handle network marketing are their friends and family. Believe it or not, your friends and family can be your worst enemy when it comes to your network marketing business. When you begin your network marketing business and you share your opportunity with them, you may have some of them join your business but the vast majority of them will not. In fact, most of your friends and family would rather see you fail than see you succeed. In most instances, if you decide that network marketing is not for you and you let your friends and family know that you are no longer in the business, they will tell you "I knew that wasn't for you" or "that was stupid of you to do that in the first place" or "I knew you couldn't do it." These are the people we refer to as your broke friends and family and they are your worst critics. Why listen to anything they have to say?

Let's say your network marketing business is successful and most of your friends and family did not join your business. Suddenly, you become their savior. You will see the greed take affect and the only thing they will see out of you is an ATM machine. The best way to handle situations like these with your friends and family is to simply say "if you need some money, why don't you take a look at my opportunity and I can show you how you can make the same amount of money I did so you wouldn't have to borrow money from me." If they say yes, great! If they say no, move on and do not give them any money. They do not want to help themselves out of poverty so they are looking to you to help them get out of poverty. Run!

An obstacle that many people cannot handle in network marketing is putting in the time and money for their network marketing business. Even though you have paid your initial investment for your network marketing business, the question comes in as to whether or not you are willing to buy the products and/or services to make your network marketing business successful? Every network marketing company has either a product, a service or both the company offers and many representatives do not purchase any of these products or services in order for their business to be successful. Why would a network marketer do that? That's like a

McDonald's franchisee not wanting to sell Big Mac's on the menu or Burger King not putting the Whopper on the their menu. As a network marketer with a business, it is imperative to know your products and services because you will have customers that will ask you questions about them and if you do not have the answers to their questions, they will not buy anything from you. In fact, the customer will believe that you are a fraud and will tell other people not to buy anything from you. The power of word of mouth is strong and if your word doesn't sell, your business will suffer. It is very important to know your products and services and to always have them on hand and readily available for your customers.

This next obstacle in handling network marketing will trip up any person. The question will remain if you can handle it. The question is would you be willing to talk to people? Many people have a hard time talking to others about anything so imagine you're in network marketing and the first thing you have to do is talk to people. The many people that are introduced to a network marketing opportunity will not do it because they do not like talking to people and that's understandable. But look at how much business they are allowing to let pass them by simply because they do not want to have a conversation with someone. Word of mouth is how many businesses have received their success. Remember many years ago, businesses like McDonald's and Burger King did not have social media to rely on to get the word out about their burgers. They had to rely on word of mouth. Talking to people is still a very effective voice in the community of network marketing and it is also a big fear to many people. In network marketing, talking to people is a must but the question you have to ask yourself if you're trying to get into network marketing is can you handle talking to people?

Next, in the world of network marketing, most companies have business opportunity meetings where they present the opportunity to would be business partners. This next question pertains to this subject and that is would you be willing to do presentations? Look, if you're in network marketing and you have never done a business presentation for your business, why are you in network marketing? This is what makes you money in your business. This is what brings in business partners. This is what brings in customers. If you are not willing learn your business opportunity presentation and present it, you need to get out of the business. Better yet, if your company offers a video that shows the presentation and you are not willing to show it, again, why are you in network marketing? This is your bread and butter, why not take advantage of this money making opportunity for your business? Isn't that what your network marketing company tells you to do in order to be successful? If you do not want to take advantage of these money making tools, you need to get out of network marketing.

This next obstacle will start stepping on some toes and this has happened so many times and unfortunately, it has happened over and over again and it is a waste of not only your time and your upline's time. It is could you handle the "30 day rule"? First of all, let's define the "30 day rule." The "30 day rule" is someone that gets started in their network marketing business and they only give it 30 days to either make their initial investment back or not. When the 30th day comes, they leave the business with or without making any money. Let's get this straight right now, if this is the only reason why you are getting into network marketing, you do not need to get started in the business. In fact, just pass it up and keep moving and let someone else who's serious about network marketing get a shot at network marketing.

Now, for those of you that have made it past the "30 day rule," the next question is could you handle the "60 day rule"? Just like the "30 day rule," the "60 day rule" means when someone joins a network marketing company and leaves the business after just 60 days in the business. Again, if you are not serious about network marketing and are only looking to make money in 60 days and then leave, do not waste anyone's time and simply do not join.

Another obstacle that faces people in network marketing is would your relationship last? Ask yourself if you were really considering a network marketing business if your marriage or relationship could really withstand the amount of time and work you would need to put into your business to become successful? Let's be honest, many people that start off in network marketing are excited and believe their spouse or significant other will be excited with them about this new venture called network marketing. What they do not realize is the amount of time the business will take to build your business. That business building will include conference calls, business opportunity meetings, and conventions. Even though your business will become successful doing these things, your spouse or significant other will believe that you are spending too much time away from them and it could lead to friction in your relationship. In some cases, it could lead to a breakup or divorce. You really need to ask yourself if you're very serious about network marketing, can your relationship handle it.

Next, if you could really handle network marketing, would you really be able to help out your business partners (downlines) if they were really putting in the effort into their business? Would you be willing to help your business partner close out a prospect for their business? Too many times, we see people in network marketing that do not help their downlines build their businesses and make sure they are following the system so they can be successful. This is what can cause friction within your own business and you can lose business partners and customers. It is very important as an upline to pay attention to your downline. If you are not willing to help your downline, you need to get out of network marketing or not even consider network marketing. If you are going to create a team, you need to be willing to work with your team.

Finally, would network marketing be beneficial for your children? If you are very serious about your future and you want to make sure you have a legacy, would network marketing be the way for you to do that for your children? If you really look at it, network marketing has created many millionaires. The question in your mind is will you be the next one? Will you be the person that will be able to leave a stable financial future for your children? That answer will depend on your mindset. That will depend on whether or not you can really handle network marketing.

Chapter 3

Are You Coachable?

What is coachable? Being coachable in network marketing is something we hear all the time but the question you need to ask yourself is are you coachable? Coachable is defined as "capable of being easily taught and trained to do something better" ("Coachable," www.learnersdictionary.com).

Here is an example of being coachable. When you start on a new job and you get on the job training on the first day, isn't that called being coached how to do your new job? It's the same thing in the network marketing world.

The company has a system in place that teaches you how to market their products and services and present the opportunity to potential business partners. The company also has materials available for you to use and teaches you how to talk to potential customers that may be interested in your products and services. Also, your uplines are available to help show you how to grow your network marketing business the right way and help show you all of the do's and don'ts of the business. This is so critical to being coachable in network marketing because if we are not willing to be open-minded and know what we are supposed to do in network marketing, you will not be successful.

The biggest failures in network marketing now are people not willing to be coachable. People have network marketing businesses but refuse to do any of the work to make it successful. They refuse to follow the system that is in place to become successful. If you are not willing to follow the system or follow anyone, you are not coachable and you simply need to get out of network marketing. Stop wasting your time and your upline's time and energy. Your upline will not come to your market and help you build your business if you are not willing to do the work. Uplines like to work with business partners they see working hard with their business to become successful. What that means is they are seeing their business partners actually putting people in the system, they are actually adding customers to the system, they are actually talking to people and they are holding business opportunity meetings on a weekly or monthly basis. Simply put, they are seeing that business partner being a leader. If you are not being a leader, not being coachable, this is not your line of work and you need to get out of network marketing.

Chapter 4

Can You Be A Success?

How bad do you want it? How bad do you want to be successful in network marketing? The bigger question you need to ask yourself is can you be a success in network marketing? If you are very serious about network marketing, the answer should be a very loud YES! If you are sitting there with doubt about being a success in network marketing but too busy looking at everyone else's success and think you cannot be the same way, why are you in network marketing complaining? Better yet, why are you in network marketing? If you want to be a success in network marketing, stop whining and get to work!

One of the first things you need to do in order to become a success is the time you frame are giving yourself to obtain success. Have a realistic time frame instead of a ridiculous time frame. Meaning, a reasonable time frame is approximately three to five years. A ridiculous time frame is one to three months. If you are looking for success in an extremely short period of time, then you are not looking to be a serious network marketer. You are trying to make a fast buck to pay off a bill really fast and then quit the business. This is not a good reason to get into network marketing. In fact, you are using the industry for a temporary fix and using people in the process for a personal agenda and not looking at network marketing as a serious business. Network marketing is not a game, it is a business. If you are not serious about it, you will be recognized as a fraud and no one will do business with you.

Another reason people are not successful in network marketing is because of excuses. Now everyone has 24 hours in the day, but why will we allow our jobs, our family life, our school life, and our kids get in the way of our success? Yes, all of these things and these people are very important in our lives but if we want success in network marketing, we cannot make excuses and put our business to the side for these things. At the end of the day, a successful network marketer never makes excuses and gets the job done and their families understand that becoming a success takes sacrifice. The question is will you allow excuses to stop you?

Next, will I allow life to take over my road to success? This is another obstacle that blocks many people in network marketing.

What do we mean by life? Life meaning a death in the family, your car breaking down, you working overtime at your job, you have suddenly taken ill or in the hospital or a loved one is in the hospital. Something in life will take effect and that will prevent you from having a successful network marketing business. Look, life happens all the time. Ask yourself this question, do you think life stopped Bill Gates from building his empire with Microsoft? Life was happening to Steve Jobs in front of our eyes but it did not stop him with the introduction of the iPhone; a product we use every day. If it did not stop these men from building their businesses to where they are today, why would you let life stop you from

building your network marketing business to

the success it can become? Can you be a

success in network marketing? Absolutely! It

all depends on your mindset and your

determination.

Chapter 5

"The Player Haters"

Here we go! Who are "The Player Haters" of network marketing? "The Player Haters" are what we refer to as the negative people that are both in network marketing and not in network marketing and they have nothing nice to say about the industry. If you are a network marketer and you have been in the industry for years, you know who these people are but a name has not been put with these people until now. We are about to recognize these "player haters" in the network marketing industry so hold on to your horses now. These are the people that are in the network marketing industry that taint the industry and they need to really consider getting out of it.

The first group of "player haters" are those people that have been in one network marketing company and failed. Then joined another network marketing company and failed again. Then says "network marketing doesn't work" but they have joined yet another network marketing company and they continue to bad mouth the industry. If you or someone in your downline is like this, cut them loose. Better yet, do not even talk to a person like this.

Pass them up and not even give them the time of day because if you do, not only will they poison other people in your downline, they will poison any person they talk to about the business. These people are unstable because they bounce from one company to the next company and every company they have been with, they have found something wrong with it. Do not connect with these people, MOVE ON!

The second set of "player haters" are the people that are in network marketing and do absolutely nothing with their business but cannot understand for the life of them why they are not making any money. Why are you in the business if you plan to do nothing with it? You are simply playing the game of network marketing and not actually working the business of network marketing deeming you a "player hater." If you are not planning to do absolutely nothing in your business but just look at it and then say "I'm not making any money," get out of the business and stop wasting everybody's time.

The next set of "player haters" are the people who are in network marketing but refuse to be coachable! They know everything about network marketing but do not have a single business partner and they refuse to follow the system. In other words, you are the upline but the business partner or "player hater" is calling you the stupid one. WHAT? You mean to tell me you do not want to learn the system, you do not want to know anything about the products or services offered by the company or you do not want to know about the systems we have in place to gather customers and business partners but you do not want our help and you know everything? Let's get this straight right now, if this is you, get out of network marketing now. You are a "player hater" of network marketing and you are an insult to the industry if you do not want to follow the systems in place for you. You do not know everything. If you knew the system the way you say you do, you would have customers and business partners. Otherwise, get out of network marketing and make room for someone that is serious about the business.

The next set of "player haters" are the people who are in network marketing and refuse to do a business presentation because they refuse to learn the presentation, they refuse to learn about the products and services offered through the company and they refuse to try any of the products or services. One question, why? This is your bread and butter of your business. Why do you not want to expand your business by doing any of these money making items? By not doing this, you are throwing money away. It also says "I don't need to make any money, let someone else who needs money more than me make it."

The next set of "player haters" in network marketing are those people in network marketing that have business partners in their downline and they bad mouth them. This is one of the worst forms of player hating in network marketing today. This causes a lot of friction between business partners and can cause you to lose customers. It goes beyond

unprofessional. It also questions your ethics

and integrity. If you are one of those uplines

that bad mouth your downline, you do not

need to be in network marketing.

The next set of "player haters" are those

people that have a prospect ready to close out

but they refuse to let their upline help them

close out the prospect. This is what we like to

refer to as the "I got this" syndrome. Why do

you believe you do not need your upline's help

in closing out a prospect? Your upline is

available to help you put new business

partners in your business in order to help you

grow your business. Not only are they helping you win but your upline is also winning. Everyone is helping everyone. The "I got this" syndrome needs to leave your mind. If it does not leave, then you are a "player hater" and you need to leave network marketing.

The next set of "player haters" are those people that are in network marketing that are all about themselves and no one else. These people have more of a mindset of "who cares about my downline, as long as they are making me money, I'm good." That is the worst attitude to have in network marketing. We are in the business to not only help see our businesses grow but to help our business partners grow and make sure everybody wins. Being selfish in network marketing is a "player hater" mindset and you need to get out of the business. It's just that simple!

Finally, this set of "player haters" are people in network marketing without any integrity. Do not claim you have worked so hard in your network marketing business when in fact you have cheated your way in your business. You may not believe this does not happen in network marketing but unfortunately, it happens. You have people in the network marketing industry that do not earn the positions they are in. They actually buy the positions and then tell their business partners they worked hard at earning their positions. That is a lack of integrity and you are actually hating the network marketing industry. If you cannot earn your position the honest way, get out of network marketing.

The next set of "player haters" are those people that are not in network marketing. The first set of "player haters" are those people who say network marketing is a pyramid scheme. This is a typical comment from people that do not understand the concept of network marketing. This is a comment made out of hate from a person after hearing from another person that has been in network marketing and was unsuccessful in the business that network marketing is a pyramid scheme. Network marketing has and always will be put in this category for all of the wrong reasons. Network marketing is not a pyramid scheme. In network marketing, you start off as the CEO of your own business and you recruit others under you to grow your business. You also offer products and services in your business. A pyramid scheme does not offer products and services. They tell you to put up your money and that's it. The problem with that is pyramid schemes are illegal. Network marketing companies offer products and services and therefore are not illegal. But, if you really pay attention to the structure of your job, it's shaped like a pyramid scheme, just in a more traditional setting that we are used to seeing but called an organizational chart. Get the proper information before going with someone with a bad taste in their mouth about network marketing.

The second set of "player haters" that are not in network marketing is a spouse or a partner that refuses to support you in your network marketing business and wants you to fail in your business. Believe it or not, this happens a lot in network marketing. You are very excited to start your new business but when you tell your spouse or partner about your business, they become angry and they want you to quit. When they see that you have not quit your business, they begin to bad mouth your business and will do anything to sabotage your business. Some will go as far as a breakup or divorce because that spouse or partner feels you are spending too much time away from them and too much time with your business. Another big reason for the non-support is a bad experience from a previous network marketing company. Your spouse or partner will feel "if we were unsuccessful with one network marketing

company, what makes you think we will be

successful with this network marketing

company?" This is hate on another level and if

you want it bad enough, the best thing to do is

to ignore the hate. Even if it means ignoring it

from your own spouse or partner. If you want

success bad enough, work your business hard

enough and you will have the success.

The next set of "player haters" that are

not in network marketing is a spouse or

partner that want to compete with you in a

network marketing company to see how many

people the both of you can get to join their

business. What is this the network marketing version of Family Feud? Network marketing is not a competition. This is a business and you need to treat your business as such. If you and your partner treat this business as a game, you will not be successful and your business partners will not be successful. It is called having morals and integrity. Do not play with other people's money and waste people's time with your games. Treat your business as a business, not a game show.

The next set of "player haters" not in network marketing are people that believe network marketing is too expensive. These people that say network marketing is too

expensive are the same people that say a

pack of gum is too expensive. Bottom line, if

you want to start your own business no matter

what it is, you will have to invest your own

money to get it started. For example, it will

cost you six figures if you want to start your

own franchise McDonalds, Burger King, or

Wendy's. In network marketing, you will pay a

cost to start your own network marketing

company. The difference is the majority of

these network marketing companies will not

have a startup cost that is six figures. Yes you

will have to buy products for your customers to

sample but if you want your business to be

successful, you will need to invest in your business. Any entrepreneur will tell you to invest in your business. A broke person will tell you network marketing is expensive.

Finally, the last set of "player haters" that are not in network marketing are those people that believe that you have turned into a snob. When you started your network marketing business, you will reach a certain level in your business. The people that you have been around for many years will believe that you have turned into someone different and will call you names like a snob. These people simply do not like the person you have turned into which is a professional business person. They would rather see you broke just like them instead of successful. Why would you pay attention to these "player haters?" It's obvious they want you to fail so why would you listen to anything they have say about your network marketing business? This is your business, not their business. When you begin your business, your true friends will show up. Unfortunately, the people you thought were your friends will disappear and not support your business. Most will even threaten you and tell you not to call them. When they tell you these things, do not associate with them. Yes it will hurt but you have to learn to move on with your life and your business. Your

success does not revolve around your friends.

Your success revolves around how much time

and energy you put into it. In the long run,

your friends will come around and they will end

up supporting up but be careful, they will

support you but for the wrong reasons. The

big reason will be because they see you have

money and they will expect you to supply them

with money. Do not supply these "player

haters" with any money. If they want to earn

money, let them look at your network

marketing opportunity so they can earn money

alongside you and the both of you can earn

money. If they say no, then ok, move on and

leave these "player haters" alone.

Chapter 6

Why Not Network Marketing?

Why choose network marketing? What's the big deal about network marketing? What people do not understand about network marketing are the many different factors that is associated with network marketing and it is all positive.

First of all, the unlimited income potential that is associated with network marketing. Did you know there are many millionaires that have been created as a result of network marketing? YES! Network marketing will give you the freedom to earn an unlimited amount of money. The income potential again depends on the amount of work you put into your business in the beginning stages. If you put in the work, the income you can make in network marketing is substantial.

With the substantial income comes financial freedom. Financial freedom is something so many people would love to achieve. Unfortunately, so many people live paycheck to paycheck and will not know how it would feel to have financial freedom. In network marketing, when you have obtained the level of success and money is no longer a problem, you have obtained financial freedom.

No more worrying about how will I feed my kids or how will I be able to put gas in my car or how can I fix my car and I have no money in my bank account. Network marketing has set so many people free from worry that many people in network marketing are showing others how to obtain the same level of success they have achieved. If they can do it, why not you?

In network marketing, you will meet lots of people in your business. You may think there are not a lot of people in network marketing but when you attend a conference and you see the number of people associated with network marketing, you become amazed with the number of people that are in the business. You become more amazed with the people that have built a successful business and have a successful network of people within their network. Events such as conferences and regional events will give you and your business the boost and information you need to be successful in your business. It will also show you that you are not alone in the network marketing world. The people you will meet at these events and throughout your network marketing career can give you knowledge on what they did to be successful and you can help each other. Always stay open and be willing to meet new people in network marketing but always beware of those people in network marketing that are trying to cross recruit you. Those looking to recruit you into their business and you already have a successful network marketing business makes them look desperate and in a lot of network marketing companies, it is against policy and it can get you terminated from the company. Do not cross recruit anyone into your business. It will hurt your business.

In network marketing, you get to travel all over and meet new people in the process. When you are building your business, you are traveling to many places and meeting people in the process. You may not have a lot of new business partners that will join your business in the same city that you live in; they may come from another city or state which would require traveling. This is how many network marketers build their businesses. Many network marketers build their business throughout the world.

Finally, have fun with network marketing. It's not about being serious all of the time. It's about going out there and having the best time you can have. Yes, there will be times that you will have some serious moments which would require you to be serious but for the most part, have fun with your business. When your business partners see your excitement for your business and the fun that you have for your company, that in turn will be for your business partners and that will turn into success. Whatever you do with your business, your business partners will do the same thing. If you're not having fun with your business and you're not excited about your business, your business partners will be the same way and your business will not be successful. Enjoy your business and be the best that you can be in your network marketing business.

Remember, have fun, enjoy your business and enjoy your success.